Darlene

Eloise Greenfield

Illustrated by
George Ford

SCHOLASTIC INC.

New York Toronto London Auckland Sydney

Text copyright © 1980 by Eloise Greenfield.
Illustrations copyright © 1980 by George Ford.
All rights reserved. Published by Scholastic Inc.
Printed in the U.S.A.
ISBN 0-590-67498-6

3 4 5 6 7 8 9 10   23   02 01 00 99 98 97

For the students at
Sharpe Health School in Washington, D.C.

and for
Alesia Ann Revis

For Tchad, Shawna,
Olivia

Darlene wanted to go back home.

Uncle Eddie said,
    "Your mama's coming to get you at two o'clock."

Her cousin Joanne said, "Come on, let's play."

But Darlene said, "I want to go home!"

"Wait until two o'clock," Uncle Eddie said.

So Darlene played a game with her cousin Joanne.

Then she asked Uncle Eddie, "Is it two o'clock yet?"

Uncle Eddie said, "Not yet."

So Darlene played another game

with her cousin Joanne.

Then she asked Uncle Eddie, "Is it two o'clock yet?"

Uncle Eddie said, "No, not yet."

So Darlene played one more game

with her cousin Joanne.

Then she asked Uncle Eddie, "Isn't it two o'clock yet?"

But Uncle Eddie said, "Not quite yet."

So Uncle Eddie played his guitar and Darlene sang songs
with her cousin Joanne, and then

the doorbell rang, and Mama was back.

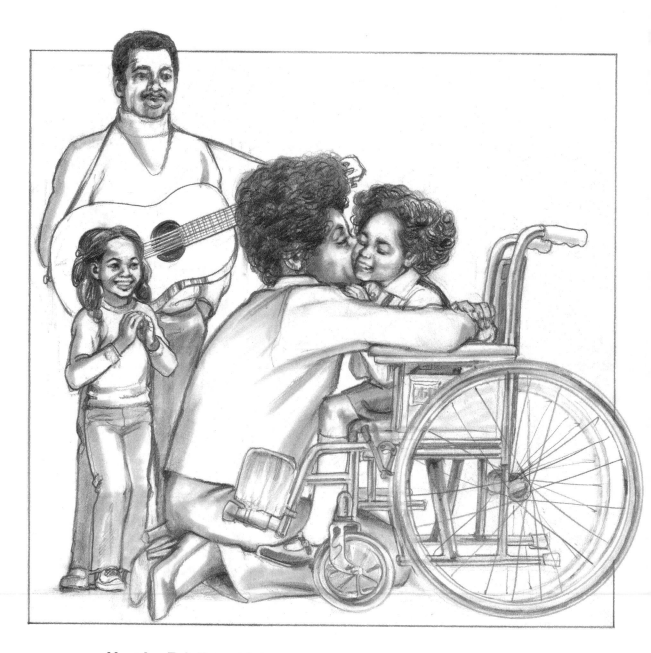

Uncle Eddie said,
"Now, Darlene, you can go back home."

Darlene looked at her Uncle Eddie
and she looked at her cousin Joanne and she said,

"I don't want to go home!"

Uncle Eddie said,
   "Darlene, you don't know *what* you want."

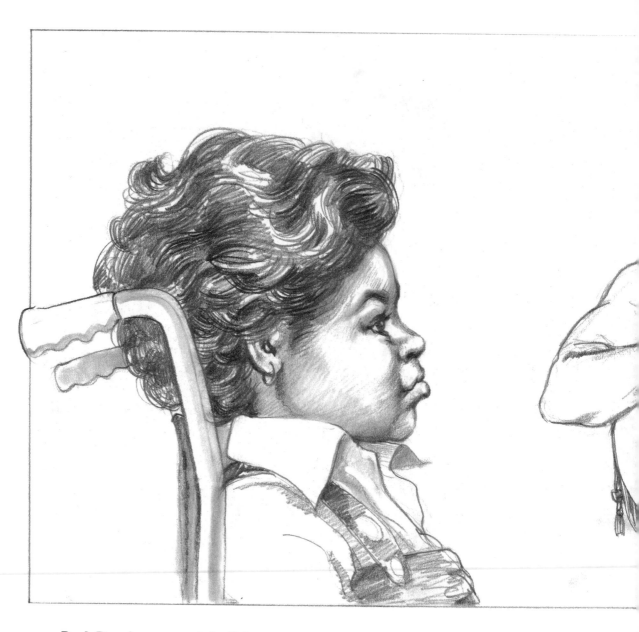

But Darlene said, "Yes, I do.
    I want to change my mind when I want to."

Uncle Eddie laughed and Joanne laughed
and Mama laughed

and then they all sat down and sang songs.

And the one that sang the loudest was Darlene.

The artist thanks Ms. Shirley Johnson, Director of the
Muscular Dystrophy Association, and Dr. Oscar H. Ciner,
Professor of Health Sciences and Director of Health Services
at Long Island University, Brooklyn Center, New York.